THE SONG SHE NEVER GOT TO SING

F.K. JADOON

AURAQ
PUBLICATIONS

Printed in the Islamic Republic of Pakistan.

Printed: October, 2022
Edition: 1st
ISBN: 978-969-749-206-0
Price: Rs 1200 PKR, $12 US

www.auraqpublications.com | raabta@auraqpublications.com
@AuraqPublications | @AuraqBooks | +92-300-0571-530
Printed and Bound by *Passive Printers* - www.passiveprinters.com

And she will forever write the song,

she never got to sing.

-F.K. Jadoon

To my mother,

whose faith in me has made me reach heights
never surmounted before.

I love you.

<u>About the Book</u>

"When the world stops listening to you, it is then that your pen starts bleeding."

The Song She Never Got to Sing is a collection of poems written on a diverse range of subjects ranging from love, longing and lies to heartbreak, anguish and betrayal.

It is the cry of a soul that never gets heard, the sigh of a lover on a cold, lonely night and the wound of a heart that never gets healed.

It is a rollercoaster that will take you on the ride of your life filled with many emotional upheavals and heartbreaking verses that will resonate inside you on a whole other level.

It is a tribute to the songs that our lips were not given a chance to sing out loud. So, dear cherished reader, it is my deepest wish that this book be a voice to all the unsung songs slumbering in your beautiful heart.

<u>Acknowledgements</u>

Thanks to the **doubts** that first greeted me when I ventured for the first time to pour my heart out. It solidified my **faith** in me more than before.

Thanks to the **discouragement** I faced when I expressed my **dreams** of reaching the **stars** and holding them in my hands. It lit my veins with an all-consuming **fire** to cradle them all in my arms and more.

Thanks to the gut-wrenching **pain** that came my way disguised as **love.** I knew to never fall a **victim** to that **imposter** again for it was not who it said it was.

Thanks to the **friendship** that made my **dead** heart **blossom** again like soothing **rain** after a **drought**. I **embraced** it with everything I was and I **believed**.

Believed in **myself** and everything that was **good** and **cherished** and **pure** in this world and I was at **peace** like one is when he knows his **soul** has finally found its true **mate.**

Thanks to the **scars** that then followed, and **destiny** intervened. It was **cunning** and it knew how to **subdue** the fire that was **raging** bright and hot. It knew if left **unattended**, I might do something as **crazy** as going after a **mirage** or embracing **what could never be.**

Thanks to all the **nights,** the **moon** witnessed a **lost battle** between what was **right** and what **should be.**

Thanks to the **words,** that then came to my **rescue** as **knights in shining armors** and have always been there like steady solid **rocks** against which I could **thrash** all I want like **angry waves** of the **mighty sea.**

Contents

Part I: *She Was Her*

Part II: *He Was Hers*

<u>**Part I**</u>

She Was Her

She Was Her

She was a fire burnt out.

A hope dying slowly in a young heart.

A flash of lightning awaiting her thunder.

She was a painting, left incomplete.

A flower, un-blossomed.

A dream, disturbed.

She was something elusive.

Like the taste of midnight.

Haunted and haunting.

Wild and proud.

She was magic.

She was her.

Cigarettes and Her

She sometimes felt she was a cigarette,

With people lighting her up,

Just to get their fill with each long drag

Of her intoxicating self.

Not caring that they were

Burning her up in the process

And turning her into ashes,

With bits of her leaving her body

In the form of smoke,

While relishing the aftertaste

She leaves behind in their sick,

Corrupted mouths.

Paradox

I am a paradox.

Beware of my contradictions.

I am fire and ice.

Darkness and light.

I am roses and thorns.

I am sweet as hell.

But bitter as heartbreak.

I am hot chocolate on rainy nights.

But vodka, on others.

I am a light drizzle.

But also a thunderous hurricane.

I can wreck and break.

Then, mend and make.

The Song She Never Got to Sing

I am a half-finished black and white sketch

Left in the attic of a seventy's manor.

But also a palette of hundred different colors

About to be splashed on an artist's wall.

I am broken

With some of my strings still attached.

I am ecstasy in its most concentrated form.

Yet, a murderous agony that only few ever experience

In their lives.

I am a hearts-and-flowers kind of girl.

And yet, someone who has lost faith

In knights in shining armors and the myth,

Called love.

I am a girl,

Who is very special, very different from others.

But I am also someone

Who can be found in the tears shed by the heartbroken ones,

And in their innocent smiles over small surprises.

I am your sweetest dream,

Yet a terrifying nightmare.

So yes,

Beware of my contradictions and me.

Cause I am a paradox,

And you're just a badly-used metaphor.

Lost Planets

We were two lost planets.

Revolving in orbits of our own,

Crossing each other every time,

Once every few hundred years.

Overlapping each other's course,

Hoping for collision, craving for the sweet chaos

To finally erupt.

Day after day... night after night...

If only to unite, in some way... any way!

Never knowing, never realizing

That our paths had long been etched into horizon,

By powers beyond our understanding.

And not once,

In all the eternity of forevers,

And the eons of infinities that separated us...

Did it ever become one!

For it was our destiny to circle around each other,

Always have each other in the periphery

Of the universe we consisted of,

But never... meet!

Home

And at the end of the day,

I always return to you.

Like birds to their nests,

And spring to barren lands.

Like the moon to falling night,

And a lost gypsy back to his homeland.

I return to you, my pain!

I return to you, my love!

At the end of every day!

At the start of every night!

Against my better judgement.

Breaking every shackle that binds me,

To everything that is not you.

I return to you, my heart!

For the only reason

That is as true as the rising sun,

And as real as this universe:

"You feel like home."

And I've always loved the feeling of it.

Whether it's the thorns that await me there,

Or the roses you so loved.

<u>Roses and Thorns</u>

I planted a rose for me

And hoped it would bear me beautiful flowers,

Which I'd love and cherish with all my heart.

But when spring came,

And every other flower bloomed,

The rose that I had planted for myself, never did.

And in its place were sharp, pointy, angry-looking thorns,

With my name engraved upon each one of them,

And hatred dripping from their ends.

A hatred so deep,

It amazed me and made me wonder,

How can a thing so beautifully created

And symbolically used for love all over the world,

Bear something that ugly, that hurtful?

But then,

The answer came to me,

Like angry waves crashing upon rocks,

That appearances are often deceptive;

And it would do me well to remember that.

- 11 -

Still, I felt a sadness so all consuming,

Settle deep within my very soul,

That it made all the happy memories I possessed turn grey,

And no smile after that could ever find its way

To my forlorn lips again!

The Girls Worth Loving

And then, there are some girls

Who are made entirely of pixie dust and dreams,

With a mouthful of happily ever afters,

They swallow every now and then,

And eyes filled with the ever shining light

Of the eternal stars.

And these are the girls

That are worth keeping and worth loving,

Because they will fill your life with colors never seen before,

And light, so intoxicating, that you wouldn't want to open

Your eyes to another light after that.

These are the girls who are always breaking inside,

But keep a smile pasted upon their lips

And a fire blazing in their eyes!

Of Caged Thoughts and Sweet Sins

My mind is a cage,

With thoughts, fluttering around, in hazy patterns.

Colliding with iron bars surrounding it.

Then, crashing back into each other.

So much so that, it is all just a fuzzy pandemonium-

A circus of this thought and that,

Jumping around,

Crashing, colliding, fighting, bickering,

Like animals, wild – left unchecked.

The space that there is, inside the cage, I mean,

Is so small, and yet always so full.

Full of every sick, corrupted thought

That can flutter and find voice,

Through that noisy, nauseous din.

I cannot make this whirling mess stop.

And it goes on, all the damn time,

With nothing but its own shrieks and screams,

Creating music and rhythm through its own reckless beats.

My mind is a mess,

Of every tragic accident that occurs,

When my hyperactive thoughts collide with each other,

Every hour of every single day.

There are also some police sirens

That always sing in the distance.

That definitely feel like my salvation in the making,

But are not, actually.

And when I listen to them, it is a sigh of relief that I heave.

Cause this bloody city of murderous thoughts,

Definitely need some law and order,

To make it stop screaming all the time.

But the police doesn't arrive.

It never really does.

And it is always only the sirens,

Adding their shrieks, to all the other shrieks,

That currently live and breathe inside me.

And so, I become deaf.

To the blaring of traffic horns,

To hideous arguments, to love songs.

Starting from the sound of my name on people's lips,

To the hollering of lifeless machines, whirring outside.

And it just so happens that,

I am a mess of magnanimous magnitude.

With my thoughts in a cage,

And my heart in a rage.

I am a hell on broken wheels.

With ashes filling its burning mouth

And smoke rising from its soot black lips.

I am a fool of my own making.

Falling prey to what should never have been,

Giving life to what only kills me!

I am duty forgotten,

Desires running rampant.

I am lips lying

And heart frozen.

- 16 -

I am shame and guilt,

Dressed as sweet sin.

<u>*The Death of a Girl Who Dreamed Too Much*</u>

And suddenly,

She stopped seeing rainbows in clouds,

She stopped believing in magic and fairytales,

There was no prince charming in her stories anymore,

Nor were there any dragons to slay no-more!

She didn't wish on falling stars or fallen eyelashes now,

And her heart didn't skip a beat, every other day now.

Her dreams now laid dead under life's stagnant pools,

And her smile was now as fake as a sad clown's painted one!

The sparkling glass in her eyes was cold hard stone now,

That saw nothing except the reflection of dark chambers

And forlorn cages, locked and shut!

And the noose that was tied around her neck that day,

Had now really begun to choke her

Like a snake slowly coiling itself around its prey!

She was now as heartless as life's many cruel jokes,

And there were no roses blooming in her dead heart anymore!

She had feared, once,

That she would one day be as cold as death come alive,

And now that she were, her heart was a frozen lake

That let no warmth inside!

At night, now she worshipped a god

That was more of a lord,

And in the day, she now posed

As whatever he'd command!

And now that, everything was said and done, after all,

All her life, the one thing that she'd always sought,

Had finally stopped evading her at last!

But it turned out that it was only ever a stupid mirage!

And that was the moment, my friends,

When she lost what was left of her faith and heart,

And her colorful dreams turned to dust, at last!

Yes, that was the moment,

When her soul died on the spot,

And her lost lonely heart,

Gave one last throb!

And then, there was silence, complete and utter, all around,

As when someone dies, and no one even comes to mourn!

The silence that no scream could penetrate,

Nor any howl could pierce!

Cause that was the day, a girl died...

Along with her dreams to touch the sky,

To wear a crown of stars, handpicked and plucked

From the clear night sky!

Yes, that was the day, a girl finally died...

Still cradling her dreams of happily-ever-afters,

And beautiful forevers in her empty arms!

That was the day, a girl died...

With a coat of adventure lining her worn out soul,

And love and poetry, finally breathing their last

Inside her hollow, hollow heart!

Un-belonged

And in the end,

It was, as if, she had never existed at all.

As if, she had just been a faded apparition,

Flitting from one place to another,

From one island to another,

Never really finding home that

She so desperately sought.

It was, as if,

She had never really belonged anywhere at all.

So that, when she moved,

From the here and now to the hereafter,

She easily slipped through the thin veil that separated them.

As if,

There was nothing and no one in the world holding on to her.

And so, in her end too,

She was left gloriously un-belonged!

Precipice

And here I stand,

On the edge of this precipice

Fearing the plunge, that will finally release me

From all ties that bind me

To the here and now,

To the doubts and insecurities,

To the troubles of yesterday

And promises of tomorrow,

That will throw me

Headlong into the land of destiny,

That has awaited me like a patient sailor,

Who faces the mighty storm,

With a firm hope, in his heart,

That the next current will surely be the last,

That the next gust of wind

Will surely calm the mighty beast,

That roars underneath the raging waves that rage on,

The crashing tides that rise and then, fall!

Sweet Lies

I feed them lies,

Carefully concocted.

Make them sip,

Hollow half-truths,

Hiding patches of ugliness,

Dust and rotten promises,

So that they wouldn't go

Near the inner broken, rustic,

House of weeds,

Hiding skeletons,

In closets,

Breathing foul,

Smell of purple oranges,

And whispered

Murmurs of the past.

Waiting, Waiting…

I stood alone in darkness,

Where there were no stars; no light to see.

Where there was no hope; no heart to beat.

I found everything broken;

Within me, around me.

While I stood there, waiting in the darkness,

All I could feel was pain and sorrows;

All I could hear were anguished cries and laments.

I didn't want to feel, didn't want to hear;

But I couldn't run away.

I had to feel, I had to hear,

For they were, a part of me.

So I felt all the pain;

Heard all the cries.

But then, after a while,

I couldn't bear it anymore.

I tried to block it out;

But there was no way out.

I called someone for help,

But none came, as ever.

So, I kept standing there;

With a bleeding heart, and a shattered soul,

Waiting, waiting...

For someone to come,

Someone to heal me.

Dead Things Stay Dead

I have a habit of carrying

Dead carcasses on my back.

Carcasses of relationships,

Dragging their heavy hides,

Carrying them upon my bent back.

Believing them to come alive someday,

When I already know that,

Nothing of the sort can ever happen.

"Dead things stay dead."

And no amount of carrying, coddling or cajoling them,

Can breathe life to what's died and gotten lost,

In the sands of time.

Stagnant

And then,

I took myself out of the race,

And became a pond of water;

Still, silent... stagnant,

Instead of a warm winding stream;

Thrashing, joyful... adventurous.

I began and ended there,

In the very same place.

And that was the end

Of a tragic tale.

Of Sins and Demons

And I lie here,

In this hell of monotonous servitude,

To powers beyond my understanding,

Awaiting my trail and sentence of sins committed,

So long ago, in innocence, in grief.

Sins, I know not of,

Yet, they seem vaguely familiar

For they remind me of a home;

A refuge, I once sought,

In nights, when demons surrounded me,

Tearing me apart with their hungry teeth - bloodthirsty,

For every last ounce of goodness I possessed.

And, in the end –

They won, like they always did.

The Last Piece of Innocence

And once again,

I feel the demons creeping in;

I see the darkness closing in!

I hear the screams deafening ears;

I see the nightmares coming alive!

I feel the horror approaching fast;

I see the shadows taking form!

I see her fight the war waging on;

I feel her will starting to crumble apart!

I see her dreams buried alive in her empty eyes,

Sticking out like sharp pointy thorns!

I feel her losing more and more of herself,

To the mighty world beyond!

I feel ice beginning to inhabit her warm heart;

I see them all trying to tear her apart!

I feel their disapproving stares,

Their ugly sneers,

Suffocating her lively spirit,

With fake smiles and crocodile tears!

I see them hungry, jaws wide open,

Big pointy teeth, waiting –

For the last luscious piece of innocence!

I feel them waiting,

I feel them wanting,

To maim, to kill!

To destroy, to ruin!

That last piece of heaven,

That last piece of innocence!

Color Blind

It was a color.

A color she had never seen before.

A color filled with the promise of life and beauty,

Love and laughter, freedom and peace.

A color she couldn't really describe in words.

A color she couldn't name or even remember having heard of.

A color filled with so much blinding light

And hope that it seemed alive –

Breathing. Living.

And it made her realize,

That she could never again settle

For any of the faded blues and greens,

Or rotten reds and yellows of this colorless world.

And if she did, or were forced to do,

Then she'd die a living death.

And she'd live a dead life.

<u>Unspeakable Thirst</u>

It just so happens that she feels thirsty,

Even after drinking the whole well.

She feels alone,

Even when she is surrounded by people.

She craves attention,

Even when she has it from everyone around her.

She feels lost,

Even when she is at home.

She feels hungry,

Even when she has just been fed all that she desires for.

But she never feels satisfied, always yearns.

For that which has always been lost to her,

For that which was never hers to call her own.

For that which is death to her, in its most tormented form.

So, she pines and craves for it, misses and seeks.

On every walk she takes, through old, cobwebbed streets,
On every journey she makes, through rusted, ruined dreams!

<u>*Left On the Outside, Looking In*</u>

I've always been left on the outside, looking in.

A mere bystander,

Standing apart from the crowd of the people

I call my own.

And yet, they are not really "mine" to begin with.

I've always been a quiet weirdo,

Trying to fathom the language people speak

And yet, not reaching their 'level of perception' at all.

It is, as if, we are worlds apart.

With eons separating us,

Filled with a deep wide chasm,

In which my voice gets lost,

Whenever it tries to glide across to them,

And whisper my heart's song lightly

Into their deaf ears.

Crushed

Her innocence laid beside her corpse,

Like crushed rose petals and several days old potpourri,

That had long since lost their luster,

Forgotten their fragrance and abandoned their beauty.

And yet, she was majestic,

In all her broken, rotten beauty!

The Fire Blazing in My Belly

There is a fire blazing in my belly,

That does not let me sit still even when I need to sit still.

A fire that is constantly burning,

Getting hotter, blazing higher with each passing minute.

A fire that is always pushing me,

To keep running towards the next big thing,

Towards the next big dream.

To make possible all that

I desire and dream, think and write about!

One that whispers to me during night's darkest hours,

That if I stop, even for a minute, I will get stuck.

And the cold, hard earth beneath my feet

Will turn into a sticky, sucking quagmire,

That will consume me ever more with each passing second.

And from which, I will never be able to get out!

So, my dear, do you see, why I never let myself stop?

It is the fear of getting stuck in places

I do not ever want to get stuck in.

And in situations, that possess the tendency to suck me in

And cut off the power supply to my spirit and drive,

Passion and love for all things that my stubborn heart clamors to do.

And it is for that exact reason,

That I keep on fanning this all-consuming fire,

And never let it die.

Because it is the one thing,

That gives me the courage to wake up every single morning,

And face all that life throws my way.

It is the absolute satisfaction I feel,

When I close my eyes every night,

Knowing that I've slayed all the dragons

That came my way in the light of the day,

And have come out the winner, as I was born to!

Heaven and Hell

I've fallen from grace,

And I've risen from ashes.

I've breathed in the starlight,

And I've bathed in the moonlight.

I've conquered my demons,

And I've embraced my darkness.

I've lived in agony,

And I've died in ecstasy.

Only to rise and fall again.

To meet you in heaven, and burn in hell!

Pink and Blue

And one day,

As I gazed outside the window,

I caught a glimpse of the sky,

And noticed that it had,

Right there, before my eyes –

Turned a brilliant shade of pinks and blues,

Yellows and greens.

The sight was so unusual,

And yet, so breathtaking -

That I marveled at the wonder

My yearning eyes beheld!

For a moment,

I could not fathom what mystery

The sky was unfolding!

It seemed like some sorcery,

Some trickery, some mockery –

And I told the sky as much!

But then I thought,

It was some potion of delight,

That the Lord was concocting.

It left me breathless and shocked,

And I felt a kick of excitement,

Right there in my solar plexus!

I was full, I was happy,

With my insides trembling with some unknown fear!

It was hidden but it was there,

And, at that time, I could not describe it in words!

That fear- now I know- it was like a snake,

Slowly uncoiling to strike!

And then, suddenly,

That it was a punch to the gut-

That beautiful pinkish blue sky-

Lost all its color, in the blink of an eye!

And I was left standing,

Under a starless sky, with the moon stolen

From my night's sky!

There was nothing there except,

A sky that now bled red,

With each flash of lightning,

And howled, with every bout of thunder!

It was as if a war had broken out,

And the only casualty there,

Were my dreams and I!

For it had now turned

Into a brutal nightmare,

And I couldn't do a single thing,

As I was standing there,

Tied with invisible strings!

So, I stood there, and watched,

The sky bleed, and the stars, turn upon each other!

I saw the moon,

With all its eternal magical glory,

Plucked from the night sky,

And thrown into the depths of the sea,

With its light going out forever!

And, then, at last,

I felt, that tiny flutter in my heart,

Take its last breath, and go still, for forever!

Untamed

There is something wrong with her heart.

It is always in open rebellion

Of the restraints put upon it,

Like a wild untamed horse,

That only desires to run free in the wilderness,

With nothing keeping it back

From following his

D e s t i n y.

The Rabbit's Hole

I tried to walk away

But as soon as I took the first step,

I found myself held back,

As though there were tight ropes,

Tying me to the leftover scraps of love,

You'd left in your wake,

And I felt my heart weighed down

By the smothering hurt,

You'd hurled my way.

And then, all at once,

I felt the earth beneath my feet open up,

And I found myself fall,

Down and down into a rabbit's hole,

But instead of finding a beautiful wonderland,

I found only a deep chasm

Filled with darkness and demons,

Waiting for me there,

With nothing but your broken promises

To chew on, every now and then,

And a cup full of concocted lies

To drink from, if I got thirsty,

As I tried, desperately, to banish

The creepy crawly creatures

That slithered up my body,

To whisper your deathly betrayal

Into my ears.

I've Stopped Looking Over My Shoulder...

I've stopped looking over my shoulder,

At the sound of every footstep that falls,

And at every sigh that is breathed across my neck.

Now, I only focus on the sounds

That please my soul and fill it with feelings

Like warm honey slowly oozing from a lightly squeezed bottle.

Now, my ears perk up only at the sounds

That matter to me,

That are close to my heart.

Like the sound of a friend's laughter,

A comforting hand falling upon my shoulder,

And the chime of every smile that graces my lips,

And then, falls to the ground,

Like slowly sprinkled rose petals.

Torment

She smiled but her eyes screamed

With the utter torment that tore her apart

And ate her up from the inside,

Slowly, silently,

Like a stealthy poison seeping inside

And working its way to its ultimate goal;

D e a t h.

Light

These cold restless nights

Are a premonition of something I've been evading;

Something that has been waiting in the dark,

For my nightmares to come out and play,

For me to cry, to give up again!

But they don't know yet,

That I've befriended light,

And this time, it's going to stay!

I Just Want One Day…

I want to fly in the endless sky,

Where every dreamer's dream breathes and resides,

Among the clouds, amid the stars!

Where there are no bounds,

No restrictions, limitations,

Just the blissful serenity of the skies!

Where the stars shine; the moon smiles,

Upon all its unsuspecting beholders, equally!

Where I can breathe the sweet scent of freedom!

Where I can drift into sweet, pleasurable oblivion!

Where I can feel whole,

Not just a walking corpse,

With a deep void, in place of a heart!

Where there is no one,

To stop, to glare, to point out the fact,

What a disappointment to share!

Where there are only flowers and colors,

Sweet-nothings and smiles!

Where I can laugh and dance,

Play and enjoy!

With no one to judge,

No one to grudge!

I just want one day… to be myself!

I just want one day… to forget who I am!

I just want one day… to fly into the sweet realms,

Of eternal peace and blissful tranquility!

I just want one day…

To finally escape to a 'land far away' –

Where there is a 'once upon a time'

And a 'happily-ever-after' waiting for me!

Kaleidoscopic Illusions

She is a lost soul,

Wandering in the maze of memories,

Where everything blurs and fades out of sight,

As soon as she thinks she has caught a glimpse

Of the forever-changing, revolving, disappearing –

Kaleidoscope of moth-eaten memories.

But their impression remains burned

On her retinas and she can no more forget them,

Than she can gouge her own eyes out.

They are there –

Illusions. Memories. Mirages.

Feeding away at her soul,

Dragging her deeper into the ever-changing maze,

Spinning a web of disillusionment around her

And tying her up in such fine threads of sweet oblivion

That she would blissfully spend her whole life

Tangled in them.

For being tangled in them,

No matter how sharp their edges are

And how often they cut into her vulnerable flesh,

Is her only fix and refuge!

My Addiction!

You are my addiction.

So sweet and tempting,

Like the aroma of my favorite meal;

That I cannot resist, or taste.

My path to self-destruction;

Like an alcoholic doomed to die,

Yet; he continues on drinking,

Knowing that it's death in itself.

My very personal alluring hell;

That I cannot stop, but to burn in,

Knowing that I'll be devastated;

Knowing that it's hell; however pleasant.

My sweetest nightmare;

That I dread; yet marvel at,

That I cannot stop hoping to see; day after day…

With an increasing passion, that burns me;

Inside and out…

My own drug that kills me;

Oh! So sweetly; silently; devastatingly,

But intoxicates me into oblivion, nonetheless,

Relieving me of the pain, though temporarily;

Ensuring that I do not part with it.

I am your addict.

And you are…. my addiction!

Unrequited

My heart is heavy!

With unshed tears and unspoken words,

While a quiet pain, stirs darkly in my soul.

Only crumbling ruins remain behind,

Of the once cherished hopes and dreams!

There is only chaos now! Everywhere!

Inside me, outside me!

Nothing remains behind;

All is destroyed, shattered, broken –

Hearts, desires, dreams!

Once again, that awful pain blooms,

Only more intense this time!

Once again, that deep, dark hole

Is wrenched open inside my chest,

Only more brutally this time!

Only one realization sighs

This terrible, tragic reality –

With each passing moment,

That my life has been changed –

Irrevocably!

All is now lost;

And it shall forever be unrequited!

The will to live, dream and breathe –

Which was once so strong;

Has now extinguished…

For forever!

Of Ashes and Rainbows

Oftentimes,

She felt the clouds rain,

Tar and ashes, soot and acid –

Upon her weary soul.

And she felt herself

Getting suffocated under the weight,

Of all that heavy, unholy shroud of emptiness.

That reminded her of nothing

But dark, dank places,

Cold, corrupted hearts,

And lost, lonely nights!

Where, once,

She had eagerly sipped

The colors of rainbow,

Only to feel them turn to

Ash in her mouth!

Ramblings of a Broken Heart

I want to scream and cry

And tear this heart out of my chest,

So that this treacherous heart of mine will never feel again!

I want to wrench my brain out of my skull,

So that no torturous thoughts will ever fill my head again!

I want to fall apart and shatter into a million pieces,

So that this agony that my wretched soul feels,

Would just leave my body!

I want to scream until my throat hurts,

And my voice becomes nothing but a harsh croak!

I want to break things with such a force,

That all my surroundings would reflect the utter chaos

That consumes me day and night!

I want to pummel my hands into walls,

So that the pain my hands would feel,

Could exceed the utter agony

That continuously cuts me down from the inside out!

I want to feel,

But I also do not want to feel!

It's hell here, inside me!

Everything is burning –

Aching – blistering – scorching!

It kills me every day, every night,

Just to stop myself from feeling, remembering, wanting!

I crave death like an addict craving for his next fix.

Just to stop this continuous, murderous pain

Consuming me all the time!

Change

Change is in the air.

I can feel it swirling around me,

Like unseen dust particles,

Floating around in fuzzy patterns,

Creating ripples across time and space.

Taking me within their thrall,

Holding me captive of the unseen future

And unchanged destiny.

Keeping me spellbound,

Wondering – anticipating – fearing -

The unknown, the inevitable!

The Noose

She was living on borrowed time,

Living each day like her last,

And yet dragging each day behind her,

As if an unwanted burden.

She was living on borrowed time,

Carrying herself from one island to another,

And yet, not really moving at all.

As if, the ship she sailed

Had stuck into a sticky quagmire

Instead of rippling water,

That had promised to take her away

To the island of freedom and dreams.

She was living on borrowed time,

With the noose getting tight around her neck,

A little more, with each passing minute,

And yet, to an outsider,

It looked like a beautiful necklace of sapphires and rubies,

Meticulously woven, wrapped around her

Slowly constricting throat.

She was living on borrowed time,

Dreading the day the executioner

Will finally pull the lever and she'd dangle,

With the whole world holding her breath and watching on,

To see her get the rightful fruit of her crime.

She was living on borrowed time,

Pretending to be someone she was not and could never be,

And yet, people cheered her on how perfectly

She performed the role they'd thrust upon her to perform.

She was living on borrowed time,

Just waiting, dreading that fateful day to come,

When she will be shackled in heavy chains

And will be made to accept them as though

An honor bestowed upon her tired soul.

She was living on borrowed time,

When all she really wanted was to cut

The string tied right around her throat,

And to just run away like a wild being,

Who knows no norms and accepts no traditions!

She was living on borrowed time,

And now, she only wanted the clock to stop,

The wind to howl, the roses to bleed

And the memories to just... burn!

<u>*The Unfurling of Her*</u>

Soft music drifted through the air ---

Made more alluring by something---

Almost magical in itself;

That lured everything,

Her --- out of its shell.

On wobbly legs,

She stumbled forward,

A little afraid, a lot skittish,

Like a newborn foal...

Not yet trusting; still doubting

The strength in her legs.

But then the magic in the air

Seemed to wrap itself around her...

Cuddling her closer...

Softly, silently...

Coercing her,

Till all her inhibitions

Faded away into nothingness...

And she became –

Something indescribable;

Like a slowly unfurling flower, seeking sunshine...

And then, she did blossom.

Like a flower... full of life!

And she danced to the soft music...

Which wrapped itself around her...

Bringing her under its spell...

She danced ---

Her hair whipping in the soft breeze...

Eyes sparkling; more radiant than the sweltering sun...

Her cheeks flushed like ripe red apples...

And in that moment, she embraced ---

All that was meant to be hers!

All that was meant for her!

For, the whole world was hers!

Full of vitality; full of life!

Silence

Silence - It was there.

A dark cloud of suffocating heaviness.

Taking me hostage again,

Of what I once had been a prisoner.

With nothing to see in front of me.

Nothing to hear.

Where there once was a chatter of laughter,

Now, the air reeked of still lifelessness.

As if, it had never witnessed and cradled, held and cherished,

Secrets breathed in the dark of the night.

With suppressed smiles,

Hearts yearning and souls aching.

For something

Unnamed – Unuttered – Unexpressed!

Silence -

Often, the best companion.

But now a haunting reminder,

Of all that was once felt,

But lost to the sands of time.

<u>*Part II*</u>

He Was Hers

He Was Hers

He was a fire blazing hot and wild.

A hope filled with purpose and promise of tomorrow.

A thunderstorm, crackling and brewing.

He was a devil incarnate.

An angel of delight. A wisp of pleasure.

A daydream come true.

He was everything she wasn't.

Everything she craved and dreaded.

Everything right and wrong.

For her.

And yet, he was hers. As she was his.

Like the moon was night's.

And the sun was day's.

Without You by My Side

I look for you in the hidden,

Dustiest corners of a colorless life.

But when I don't find you there,

I die a little more, one breath, one heartbeat at a time.

I make my way through life, like a blind man

Seeking his way through darkness.

Crashing into things,

Getting bruised by falling

Onto glass-sprinkled ground;

Hands bloodied by getting scraped,

Body aching from the struggle.

Without you by my side,

Life is nothing more than a

Deep, dark, drowning dungeon of despair.

Without you by my side,

Life is a horrifying nightmare,

From which I can never make myself escape.

Without you by my side,

I am a soul-less body seeking its host,

Not knowing, where to look.

Without you by my side,

I am a lost creature,

Mourning the loss of its true mate.

Without you by my side,

I am a tormented wolf, howling deep into the night,

Calling out for his unrequited love to the moon.

Without you by my side,

I cease to exist and slowly fade into nothingness.

Without you by my side,

My mornings don't shine and the nights never end.

Love Looked Pretty On Me

Love looked pretty on me.

But now, it doesn't.

Now, it is just dark and twisted,

With its strings lying loose,

Trailing behind me, upon damp muddied earth.

Now, it is just something dead,

With its rotten smell permeating the air around it,

Letting everybody know,

That yes, once it had been alive and fragrant!

That yes, once it had, in fact,

Looked pretty on me.

But now, sadly, it doesn't.

Oh yes, it had, looked pretty on me,

Oh how, it had looked pretty on me!

It made my heart go –

Thump-thump, thump-thump –

The first time it visited me,

But now, it doesn't.

Now, it is all dead inside.

With an eerie silence haunting the halls of my dead heart.

Now, it is a complete ghost town in there,

Where nothing breathes, no one comes, ever!

It is all just forgotten and gone, dead and silent!

Love indeed looked pretty on me, I tell you,

With its silly smiles, and twinkling eyes –

That is why, now that it has left –

There is a permanent autumn sleeping upon my lips,

And a long night nesting inside my eyes!

Spring after Rain

Give me your darkness,

Give me your pain.

Give me a chance,

To prove to you again!

That I need you like air,

I crave you like wind.

You are the dream,

That I once held in my hands!

Give me your faith,

Give me your name.

You are the love,

That I had searched for,

Time and again!

Love,

I need you to know,

That on spring days and autumn nights,

You had come to me in a splash of colors,

But I was too color blind!

You had come to me

In verses, that I could not decipher,

Nor knew the language, in which they were uttered!

You were there,

Every minute of every day,

When I ached and when I raged!

All that time,

Tucked safely between my heartstrings,

Slowly coming awake!

You filled my heart with warmth,

And shattered the ice coating its outer walls,

And so, I was, forever changed!

The Forgotten Kingdom of Memories

And I can tell you this,

With as much surety as the eternal sun,

Has of rising every morning,

That these feet that walk so eagerly everywhere,

Will refuse to take another step forward,

If they ever encounter yours in their path again.

And these empty eyes,

That dared to dream those lost dreams of you,

Will surely refuse to blink,

If they saw even a shadow of your reflection

In them ever again!

And this wild, wild heart,

That keeps fluttering its restless wings

Against the bars of the cage,

Where I have so painstakingly locked it in,

Will no doubt perk its dainty little ears up and listen,

With its galloping beat coming to a complete standstill,

If it ever heard even a single thrum of yours,

Anywhere in the near vicinity!

And this,

My dear departed one,

Is the only truth that resonates inside me,

Every hour of every single day,

Like a deathly reminder,

Trying to make its way past

The forgotten kingdom of memories.

The Other Side

I have been to the other side.

I have flown into sparkling colors,

And have landed on my stomach

On hard concrete floors.

I have tasted sunshines and rainbows,

And have witnessed them obliterate into nothingness,

Right there, before my sinful eyes.

I have written love songs and poems,

But have seen my words turn upon each other,

To tear each other apart and lie there in a bloody scrawl,

Upon innocent blank pages.

I have drunk from the fountain of love,

But have felt its pure essence turn into poison,

As soon as it touched my parched lips.

I have cradled galaxies of stars in my arms,

And then, have felt them disintegrate into smithereens,

Of all that was once bright and holy,

Leaving behind a mighty darkness,

That could rival a black hole's.

I have weaved dreams of forever,

And have seen them turn into nightmares,

With nothing but oblivion as their willing occupant.

I have relished subduing the fire,

That others seemed so weary of,

But have seen it turn into a fiery beast,

That swallowed me whole,

Leaving behind a burning mess of me,

Scattered carelessly upon the floor.

I have wished for the moon and stars,

But have witnessed them fall from my sky,

At the slightest nudge of reality and betrayal,

That pushed me deeper into complete darkness,

Blinding me to all other lights after that,

For all eternity!

The Curse That Is You

And there I was, standing –

Right where you had left me,

So many years ago.

Going through everything,

That we had done together.

Sifting through conversations,

Both happy and sad,

Joyful and teasing,

Liberating and suffocating.

Leafing through page after page of words,

Both said and unsaid, uttered and unuttered.

Listening to the flutter of those newly budded,

Newly awakened feelings.

Taking flight into the night sky,

Not bothering to fear,

The thunder and lightning,

And the utter chaos,

Awaiting them.

There I was -

Thinking, aching, agonizing -

Over what had been lost and forgotten now.

And there you were,

Still the same, after so many years.

With the same hint of that damned sadistic streak,

Flashing in your lying eyes.

Reeling people in,

Making them your playthings!

Only to leave them behind,

Once you had had your fill!

But not as they were before.

But changed, altered –

In a way that could not be undone.

You left them more,

Broken, shattered, enslaved –

To the pain of the worst kind.

The kind that ripped you apart-

And burned your insides-

From poison that spewed from memories,

That you had cursed them with.

The kind that only came with a heart so battered and broken,

That the splinters of those long cherished dreams,

Pierced and cut your insides, each time you tried to breathe,

Each time that wretched heart of yours, pumped to beat.

The kind that never lets you up for air,

But chokes and smothers you so much,

That you are left gasping for air,

Like a slowly drowning man.

The kind that kills you,

And makes you want to kill yourself,

At the same time, a hundred times, during the day.

The kind that freezes up your insides -

So much so, that ice now slithers through your veins,

Instead of warm blood,

Turning it into a tomb,

Of what once was and what could never be.

- 84 -

Yes.

There you were.

The curse that I had chosen for myself,

To live and die with,

To love and mourn for,

An eternity.

The Wild Beast

Lately,

You have been shining

Through every crack and crevice

Of my worn out soul.

And

I can no more hide you

Inside my tightly locked, well-guarded

Heart compartments.

For you have broken free –

A wild beast running rampant,

Through the dense forest

Of my barren soul.

Mighty, exultant, triumphant - in his power,

Claiming, possessing, marking - Everything as his own!

Echoes of Your Screams

Tears flow from my eyes

And leave their wet trails behind,

Like footsteps in snow.

They get erased but their essence lingers,

Which bites into my cold flesh,

With aching blue sharp bites

And I feel their presence as if a foreign intruder

Has taken refuge beneath my pale skin.

They claw at my already mutilated flesh with their sharp talons,

So that it bleeds the poisonous acid of your memories,

Which fills me up with its toxic fumes and makes me choke.

I cannot hide from them.

My throat gets clogged

And my insomniac eyes tear up.

My soul is a haunted house of memories,

And this heart is a hellhole,

Filled to the brim with writhing fires and lava

Of pain and torment,

Where naughty demons play hide and seek.

They laugh their demonic laugh at me,

Mocking me with their freaky presence,

Reminding me of what I lost and how weak I was

And still am, to this day.

I cannot banish them from their self-acclaimed home.

For, if I do that,

There wouldn't be anything left of me inside my own self,

And I would just be a hollow body,

With echoes of your screams reverberating through its walls,

Every now and then.

Albatross

She wears her memory of you around her neck,

Like the metaphorical albatross from so long ago,

Which has her wrapped in a suffocating shroud of loneliness,

That lets nothing inside,

Except icy whispers of winds,

Carrying dark omens

And the curse of carrying an agonizing past

Into the future,

To grant it a lifetime of eternity

And a promise of forever.

The Cacti of Your Memories

I walk amid paths

Strewn with the cacti of your memories.

Which stay still, strong, silent.

But there. In my path.

So that, if I want to go forward,

I have to go through them.

But when I try do that,

I get pierced by their sharp pointy thorns.

It is, as if, they do not want me to go forward.

And I remain stuck there, tangled in them.

With their thorns embedded in my body.

Where, once again,

I feel the poisonous essence of you

Seep into my bloodstream

And make its way to my heart.

Where upon reaching,

It hollers a shout of triumph

At the fact that the original owner

Of this bruised and broken heart

Has finally returned home.

And this time,

I might not get so lucky

In banishing it to the land,

Of the forgotten and the lost.

Where betrayals walk in daylight.

Where lies hold their court at midnight.

Where truths are punished at dawn.

And where, naive hearts get trampled on.

And served, on silver platters,

To the bloodthirsty, at dusk!

The Parallel Opposites

Two lost souls, burdened by past.

Floating in the river of time.

Trying to make themselves believe,

In things they've long lost faith in.

One a dreamer, the other a realist.

Hence, often a war between nightmares and dreams.

Parallels in some ways, opposites in others.

A strange, sweet balance of sanity and craziness.

Both a little troubled, both a little forgotten.

Planting their dying roses, on the imprints left by autumn.

Both a little lost, both a little strayed,

From the path that was, for them, so long ago laid!

The Sun in My Life

He was the sun in my life.

Brightening my day,

When it grew too dark with looming clouds

Of melancholy and nostalgia.

Warming my shivering body

When I got too cold from the ice,

Running through my veins.

Soothing me

With his warm balmy presence,

Whenever I grew too restless or edgy.

And yet;

Burning me alive

With his blistering hot rays,

Whenever I dared to get too close.

He was the sun in my life.

So close to me that I could feel

The caress of his eyes as they rested upon me.

And yet, so far,

That I could not even imagine

Travelling the eons and light years that separated us.

He was the sun in my life.

So remote, and yet so proud,

In his self-chosen aloofness.

His Rose

She was a rose,

Kept between the pages

Of his favorite book.

One, he watered every day,

By reminiscing the time,

She had blossomed royally

Between his arms.

And one, he lost

To the thorns of life,

That sprouted angrily,

One unfortunate day,

And took her away,

To the barren lands of death,

Never to return!

<u>Once Bitten, Twice Shy</u>

It was a day,

Like any other day.

And I was faced with a decision to make.

To choose between the stars, that I so loved to gaze upon,

And the moon, that I was already so enamored of.

But I chose the sun,

Which was never even in the equation, at all!

I chose the sun and I became his.

He warmed my soul and brought laughter back,

To the lands forlorn.

He made my heart thaw,

Where once it was, all frozen and raw!

And I loved to bask,

In the heat of his steady regard!

It was then that I realized,

That I was the real "I",

Whenever his light shone upon,

The kingdom of my plight!

And then,

I bloomed and I blossomed,

With a smile on my lips, and a skip to my step,

With a twinkle, adorning my eyes!

I was happy, I was smiling!

It was beautiful and yet, so bizarre!

And then, one day, that dark, dreadful day,

The sun I so cherished, went cold and all dark!

I asked him what it was.

And he said what he should never even have, thought of!

He asked the unthinkable,

The impossible, the undoable!

He asked for what had long died,

Leaving behind a cold, empty spot!

And the night that then fell,

After my sun's fire extinguished,

It was somehow more powerful than the last!

It left in its wake,

The death of all the merriment and joy,

That had once blossomed in my lost lonely heart!

And I was, once again,

Lost like a kite, drifting aimlessly in the vast sky,

Towards no real direction, at all!

And then,

I thought and I thought,

And I came to this conclusion, after all!

That he would definitely have known,

If he knew me at all;

That once bitten was always twice shy!

It was the rule of the burnt and lost!

I Saw You in My Dream Again

I saw you in my dream again.

And I felt that all too familiar, soul-tearing ache

In this numb heart of mine again.

And that's when I knew;

That you still had the power to wrench me open and make me bleed,

As if, I have been cut with a thousand blades all over my body,

By the mere glance of your cruel, indifferent eyes.

The eyes that had made me dream

Of fairytales and happy endings.

And the eyes, that, in the end,

Gave me nightmares of misery and disaster,

Tragedy and pain, only!

The Curse of the Love Gone Bad

Each day,

I lay my demons to rest.

Each night,

They come back to haunt me.

And I lie there,

Waiting with bated breath,

To have them deliver

The final blow,

That would release me

From this hollow existence,

And put an end,

To that which hurts all the time –

Once and for all.

But the blow never comes.

The wait doesn't end.

And the torture continues.

Till it leaves me seeping blood

On pristine white tiles,

Till every scar and wound I've ever had,

Gets scratched open again,

And I lie there,

Numbed to my very bones –

Accepting the agony for what it is:

The curse of the love gone bad.

The Fallen Angel

He was an angel,

Full of frustration and wrath.

And the world he lived in

Had never dared, at all,

To silence the mighty ocean,

That, inside him, thundered and throbbed!

He crashed and he burned,

With the things, he had left undone,

With the words, he had never said.

And the tears, he never shed.

He tried but he failed,

To soothe the angry beast,

Full of deep hurt and agony,

Disguised as fury!

He thrashed and then crashed,

Into things that he smashed!

And howled with the pain of the past,

And dreams, left unfulfilled!

He grew restless and mad,

The more he became sad,

With the rise and fall,

Of the rolling summer tide!

Yes.

He was an angel.

But not of light.

He was an angel, fallen!

Full of anger and wrath,

And all hurt pride!

Missing You...

Missing you,

Is having a hundred knives cut through me,

With their sharp pointy edges.

Missing you,

Is having my breath cut short,

When I am reminded of your dark fathomless eyes.

Missing you,

Is a torture that seeps me,

Of every drop of blood I possess.

Missing you,

Is being burnt at stake,

Where your memories act as gasoline to the fire.

Missing you,

Is aching for you in the deepest, darkest

Parts of the night.

Missing you,

Is cursing you every hour of every single day,

While praying that you be safe and sound,

Wherever you stay.

Missing you,

Is hating myself and loving you,

With every breath these treacherous lungs take.

Missing you,

Is salt being sprinkled upon

Open, bloodied wounds.

Missing you, is loving you,

When there is no love left in me to give.

Missing you, is mourning you,

While you are still alive.

Missing you,

Is experiencing loss in its worst form,

Knowing that you are now as lost to me, as am I.

Missing you,

Is slowly killing myself while resurrecting you,

One damning memory at a time.

Missing you,

Is a prayer, to put an end to the torture

I gladly welcome and accept.

Missing you, is pining for you,

The way two parallel railway tracks do,

Going together, hand in hand, towards their destination,

But never meeting, not even once,

No matter how far they go,

Or how much they yearn

For that!

Flesh and Bones

I want to

Crawl inside your body,

Make a home of your bones,

Held together,

By the strong sinew of muscle,

And just bury myself

Beneath your warm flesh,

So that the icy winds of reality

Would never reach me.

Love, Gone the Way It Came

Love,

It came on silent feet,

And a beguiling smile reeking of roses,

Rainbows and happily-ever-afters,

Playing upon its lips.

And left,

The way it came.

Stealthily.

Like a thief running away into the night,

After robbing someone of something precious.

Love, it went on its merry way.

As if it was never there before.

Stealing her smile, her dreams, and her faith.

Leaving behind a mighty chasm

Of nightmares, emptiness and heartache,

That sat upon her chest

And froze her from the inside.

Extinguishing the fire of hope

That had once burnt so bright,

And that, now,

Died, oh, so magnificently!

That it felt as if it had never burned,

Never warmed her soul,

In cold merciless nights at all.

The Puppet and the Master

I was a puppet,

In the hands of my master.

He twisted me this way and that,

Made me tumble and fall!

He had the control,

I had willingly surrendered,

So he made me dance,

To the tune of his thoughts!

And I had never before been,

So utterly distraught!

But I did as he wished,

And I did as he bid,

Cause he was my master,

And I, only a disaster!

Waiting to happen,

To erupt into chaos!

To rise and then, fall

Like the symphony of a tragic opera!

To bleed and to wail,

At life's many unjust tales!

So, he took me under his wing,

And made me forget,

That I was only a lifeless puppet,

And he, my lord!

But he was more than that,

A manipulative sadist,

Who made me fall,

For his charismatic charm!

And I fell, how I fell!

Like a house of cards,

Like perfect downy snowfall!

<u>*Come To Me*</u>

Come to me as a dream,

Or a reverent prayer upon my lips!

Come to me as a soft sigh,

Or a blessed whisper upon the wind!

Come to me in any way,

But come, you must, my dear!

For these lips are very thirsty,

The way a desert is, without the rain, all year!

<u>Weakness</u>

Loving him meant accepting my weakness,

Again and again and again.

Accepting that,

He was the rain to the desert of my soul.

That no matter where I go or what I do,

I will always be thirsty for him.

That only he was the one

Who could bring light to the darkness of my being.

And only in his heart,

Will I always find my home.

___Will you?___

Will you come to me,

And lift this block of ice from my heart?

So that it could once again sprout flowers,

Like it used to before.

So that it could get drunk on the colors of Spring,

Once again.

So that it could breathe fire and love _love_

The way it used to before.

Will you ever free me from the hold

My demons have over me?

Or do I have to do it myself?

Like I have been doing since forever.

When Autumn came uninvited and spread its wings

Upon the kingdom of my happiness and mirth,

And blocked out the only Sun,

I had ever let shine upon me.

Drenching everything

Into a frozen well of despair and anguish.

<u>Caught</u>

He kept chasing me.

As if I wasn't already caught.

In his web of lies,

By his deceptive eyes.

In his beautiful world of make-believe,

By his pretty promises, and sunny smiles.

I had started to dream,

Which had led me to believe,

In happy endings, forevers, rainbows and peace.

Never knowing, never believing

That I was heading down a path,

Where only heartbreak and misery thrived!

Breadcrumbs

I leave him small breadcrumbs,

On the trails I follow,

When I wander far,

Into the cobwebbed maze of his memories.

So that, he could follow them, if he wishes,

And find me, if he can.

To bring me back,

To the light that I am seeking,

To show the colors that are now,

Hidden from my gaze.

To reveal the wonders,

That are concealed,

To sew the wounds,

Still unhealed.

He never follows me though.

And so, the bread crumbs, I leave for him,

Get eaten by hungry birds of prey!

The light that I am seeking,

Disappears once again!

The colors, still hidden,

Go a permanent blue and grey!

And the wonders remain concealed,

From my blind gaze!

The wounds, unsewn, now fester and seep,

Poison instead of blood, turned purple and green!

And I walk and walk,

Through cobwebbed old streets,

Awaiting my tormentor and savior,

Slowly forgetting me!

Queen of His Heart

He could feel her slithering,

Deep into his body,

Running through his veins,

As one with blood,

Embedding herself deeper inside his soul.

Taking possession of his heart,

While sitting upon the throne

Perched upon the fragile strings of his heartbeats,

Ruling over the kingdom

Of his entire being,

Bringing him to his knees at last,

Like the queen she was always meant to be.

Don't You Know?

Don't you know how hard it is?

Don't you know how I ache?

Don't you know how it tears me apart,

Knowing that I cannot have you, after all?

Don't you know you are all I ever wanted?

Don't you know you are my dream come true?

A dream that I had never ever

Let myself to believe in.

Don't you know I had never even considered the possibility

That you'd exist some day?

Don't you know, how it kills me,

To know that you exist in the same universe that I do,

But also to be certain of this deep tragic reality,

That your world and mine can never be the same!

Don't you know what agony I feel,

To know that you are forever lost to me!

Don't you know how my heart breaks into tiny, little splinters,

When you say that you love me and I cannot say it back?

Don't you know how dark and haunting my nights are,

When my soul cries out for you,

And I cannot quash the yearning,

That takes root in my stupid, stupid heart?

Don't you know how I yearn,

To just be with you, to hear your hearty laughter,

To see your eyes crinkle and soften –

With love and wonder and mischief and delight!

The Desert Warrior

He was a desert warrior,

Having sandstorms at his mercy.

And she was a porcelain china doll,

A little fragile, a whole lot vulnerable.

One who could not weather his storm of a nature.

So, when his mighty winds blew her way,

She fell and shattered into a million pieces,

And he was left to pick them up, piece by fragile piece,

With regret spilling a bitter taste into his mouth.

But with each broken piece,

A little more of his haughty soul died,

And he became more of a sand-castle,

Than of a sandstorm.

Come, Fall Upon Me

Come, fall upon me,

Like rain from tumultuous clouds,

And wash the filth and grime

Of all the years passed!

Where I was hunted and haunted,

By nasty demons from the deepest depths of hell.

Coming in contact with them has marred

Not only my body but also the soul within!

Come, fall upon me,

Like rain from tumultuous clouds,

So that the blood I spilled years ago,

Might be washed away from the hands that still carry

The imprint of that foul, disgusting past.

So that the shadows may slowly fade away

And give way to pure, brilliant light.

So that, I may smell the familiar scents

That remind me of home, again.

A home filled with dancing echoes

Of love and laughter and peace;

Ah, yes… sweet eternal peace!

Come, fall upon me

And free me from the past!

Come, fall upon me

And make me whole again!

Transformation

And then, the day came,

That dark, dreadful day that we had feared for so long.

And when it did,

Everything changed,

Everything came to an end.

But it was already 'written'

That it had to end, that it will end,

Because it was never 'destined to happen' after all!

You became just a name in so many names.

A bittersweet memory, in so many memories.

But unlike all the names, all the memories,

You left a mark upon my soul,

Somewhere very deep inside me.

Every word, every feeling,

You etched them on the horizon of my being,

And I transformed.

Just like an ugly caterpillar transforms

Into a beautiful butterfly.

There was nothing left of my old self anymore,

Because "I" was not the same as before!

You had torn me open

And then sewed me back together again,

Into such 'unknown' intricate patterns,

And my parts were stitched so differently now,

That I could not fathom the 'transformation'

That took place inside me.

You were the 'transformer' of my being,

The catalyst that brought me to my own 'end'!

To The Infinity and Back...

The sound of your heartbeat,

I would die to hear it thumping beneath my ear,

As I slowly drift away into the land of dreams.

And that sleepy smile that kisses your lips

As you come back to wakefulness,

I would give all the smiles from my own,

Just to see yours the first thing in the morning.

For I love you.

I love you past sanity and pride.

I love you past eternity and forever.

I love you to the infinity and back.

The Poisonous Remains of Your Love

My heart is not in the right place today.

It seems to be lodged somewhere between my ribs and throat.

Cutting my air supply while pressing on my windpipe.

Suffocating me with its crushing weight.

A heavy weight placed upon my chest.

Blocks of guilt.

Regret.

With some of the

Poisonous remains of your

L o v e.

<u>Letting You Go</u>

And

I find you

Slipping away from me.

As if, the hold my heart and brain

Had over your memories,

Is no longer strong enough

To give life to them.

You are now just an unpleasant spot

On an otherwise clean slate.

Nothing more.

Touch

My fingers ache to touch your essence

One more time.

The absence of you is a torture,

They cannot bear.

And the memory of you is a loss,

They cannot get themselves accustomed to.

But how can they miss an essence,

That they have never touched?

And how can they reminisce a touch,

That they have never felt?

<u>*Chocolates and Your Name*</u>

You know,

Your name used to be my favorite.

I used to savor it as it rolled off my tongue

Almost as much as I savored consuming

My favorite chocolates.

But now,

It feels like acid burning my insides,

Leaving only a bitter and rustic taste behind,

One that I try to rinse off,

Repeatedly,

By sipping your broken promises,

And chewing all the rotten feelings,

You vowed to possess.

A Slave of Darkness, Bound to the Light

She was starlight,

He tried to capture in his arms.

And every time he tried to do so,

She slithered away from him a little more,

Cause she was a goddess of light,

And he, a mere being of darkness.

So he fell, and he fell,

A little more under her spell,

Till there was nothing left more than a shell,

Of the person he once was, and the one he became,

A slave of darkness,

Bound to the light!

Rains of Your Memories

And in some nights,

Your memory is a light drizzle,

That falls upon my weary soul,

And dampens it a little.

While in others,

It is a constant downpour

From angry thundering clouds,

Wetting me to the skin,

And drenching me whole.

And it is during these nights,

That it feels as if I would not survive

This flood of your memories,

And would surely be drowned in the sea of it,

Before sunrise come next morning.

Hide and Seek

What tears they are?

What laments the darkness cradles?

What cries I hear,

In the whispers of the wind?

Who cries in the night?

Who mocks and laughs?

Who scrapes bloodied nails,

On the edges of time?

Is it you or me?

Or the shadows I see?

Around every corner,

Playing hide and seek!

Toxic

Toxic fumes in the air,

Blistering hot sun scorching skin,

Poisonous thoughts creating halos,

Fuzzing bees of lost memories,

Stinging; again and again!

Love draped promises;

Sugarcoated,

Betrayal peeking from the shadows.

Drawing, beckoning, tempting, mocking!

Chaos approaching;

Mind numbing, heartbreaking,

Clashes of wills, murder of dreams.

Corrupted, corrosive, suffocating, piercing!

Where Does a Word Go, after Getting Erased?

Where does a word go,

After getting erased?

Where does a sigh go,

After getting heaved?

Where does a moment go,

After getting spent?

To the realm of infinity.

To the land of impossibilities.

To the kingdom of dreams.

Unachievable

So many words remain unspoken,

So many desires remain unexpressed,

So many prayers remain unanswered, unheard.

Only regret remains…

Only tears and sorrow… loss and agony,

Of the unachievable…

Only emptiness resides,

Inside hollow eyes, and soul-less bodies…

No beating heart, no breathing soul, only emptiness…

Just this deep, dark, writhing chasm;

Full of emptiness!

Only anger remains,

Only rage burns inside blackened hearts.

Only challenge beats in every pulse, every beat

To take, to conquer, to win … against destiny!

But has anyone ever won against fate?

Against the life force,

That makes and then breaks?

Against the eternal power,

That gives and then takes?

No one, not ever!

Printed and Bound by *Passive Printers* - www.passiveprinters.com
Printing press that offers Print on Demand (POD) Facility.
Printed in The Islamic Republic of Pakistan.